JUNIOR BIOGRAPHY FROM

# ANCIENT CIVILIZATIONS

# GENGHIS KHAN

## JOHN BANKSTON

Mitchell Lane
PUBLISHERS

P.O. Box 196
Hockessin, Delaware 19707
Visit us on the web: www.mitchelllane.com
Comments? Email us: mitchelllane@mitchelllane.com

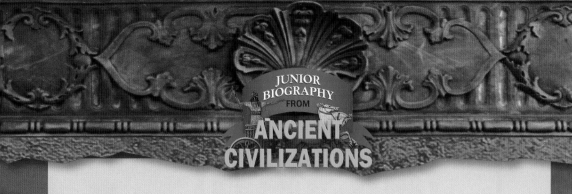

# JUNIOR BIOGRAPHY FROM ANCIENT CIVILIZATIONS

Alexander the Great • Archimedes
Augustus Caesar • Confucius • Genghis Khan
Homer • Leif Erikson • Marco Polo
Nero • Socrates

Copyright © 2014 by Mitchell Lane Publishers

Printing   1   2   3   4   5   6   7   8   9

**ABOUT THE AUTHOR:** Born in Boston, Massachusetts, John Bankston began writing articles while still a teenager. Since then, over two hundred of his articles have been published in magazines and newspapers across the country, including travel articles in *The Tallahassee Democrat, The Orlando Sentinel,* and *The Tallahassean.* He is the author of over eighty books for young adults, including biographies on Alexander the Great, reporter Nellie Bly, scientist Stephen Hawking, author F. Scott Fitzgerald, and actor Jodi Foster.

**PUBLISHER'S NOTE:** The facts on which the story in this book is based have been thoroughly researched. Documentation of such research can be found on page 45. While every possible effort has been made to ensure accuracy, the publisher will not assume liability for damages caused by inaccuracies in the data, and makes no warranty on the accuracy of the information contained herein.

Library of Congress
Cataloging-in-Publication Data

Bankston, John, 1974–
 Genghis Khan / by John Bankston.
    pages cm. — (Junior biography from ancient civilizations)
 Includes bibliographical references and index.
 ISBN 978-1-61228-432-3 (library bound)
1.  Genghis Khan, 1162–1227—Juvenile literature. 2.  Mongols—Kings and rulers—Biography—Juvenile literature.  I. Title.
 DS22.B3227 2013
 950'.21092—dc23
 [B]
                                        2013012554

**eBook ISBN:** 9781612284941

PLB

# CONTENTS

Phonetic pronunciations of words in **bold**
can be found on page 46.

Raised without a father in extreme poverty, the boy known as Temujin grew up to rule the largest empire in history as Genghis Khan.

# CHAPTER 1
# Young Love

When **Temujin***  was nine years old, he wasn't worried about math problems or spelling words. He was worried about finding the perfect wife.

The girl he chose was a year older. Their fathers thought they had fire in their eyes and light in their faces. They believed the pair would be famous together. They were right.[1]

Temujin's father **Yesugei** was the head of a group of Mongols called a clan. Temujin's mother **Hoelun** had come from a different clan—Yesugei decided that he could find a good wife for his son from Hoelun's clan.

A lucky accident occurred. As Yesugei and Temujin headed to meet with members of Hoelun's clan, they met a girl named **Börte** and her father. It was love at first sight.

The match seemed perfect. The girl was from the same clan as Temujin's mother. Her parents asked Temujin to stay with them and Yesugei agreed. He gave them his horse. Then he asked them to keep the family pets away from Temujin because, "my son is afraid of dogs."[2]

*For pronunciations of words in **bold**, see page 46.

**Although many marriages in Mongolia were arranged before the couple even knew each other, Börte met her future husband when she was only ten years old.**

While Temujin got to know his future wife and her family, his father rode away. Temujin never saw him again.

The trek home took three days. Along the way, Yesugei came upon a group of Tartars. Although he often fought with Tartars, he stopped at their camp and shared their meal. Shortly after returning home, Yesugei died. It was believed that the Tartars had poisoned his food.

When Yesugei died, Temujin became the leader of his clan. But the adults were not interested in listening to a boy. So they took the clan's livestock and left. Temujin was marked for death. But he survived.

Temujin grew up poor in one of the most brutal places on the planet. As an adult, he was one of the richest men who ever lived. He controlled an area almost twice as big as the United States. The lands that he ruled were located in today's countries of Mongolia, China, Russia, Iran, North Korea, and **Kazakhstan**.

His enemies feared him. His soldiers loved him. They honored Temujin by calling him their "king of kings." They called him Genghis Khan (JENG-gis KAHN).

# The Secret History of the Mongols

The Secret History of the Mongols is the oldest surviving book about Genghis Khan. The author is unknown, but was probably someone close to the ruler. Some believe the book was written by **Shigi,** an abandoned Tartar boy raised by Hoelun as Genghis's brother. He grew up to be a judge and general.

Written around 1240 CE, the book is a history of the Mongol leader and his family. It also describes life in Mongolia eight hundred years ago.

The events in The Secret History of the Mongols took place a few decades before the book was written. The Mongols had just begun writing. Although Genghis Khan did not read or write, he had a written language created so his orders could be read.

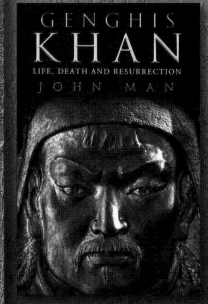

Modern writers who want to tell the story of Genghis Khan often use The Secret History of the Mongols. "It rings true because it portrays the bad along with the good," author John Man explains in Genghis Khan: Life, Death, and Resurrection.[3]

It is the story of a boy named Temujin. He was afraid of dogs and lost his father, but he grew up to rule an empire.

Temujin was born at the site known as Delüün Boldog near Burkhan Khaldun Mountain and the Onon and Kherlen Rivers in modern-day northern Mongolia, not far from the current capital, Ulaanbaatar.

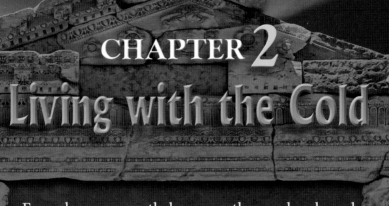

# CHAPTER 2
# Living with the Cold

Few places on earth have weather as harsh and unforgiving as the Steppes. Stretching across Central Asia, it is a place with few trees and little rain. Farming is almost impossible there.

Temujin's birthplace lies in northeastern Mongolia, north of China and south of Russia. One writer described the region as "a field the size of a small country."[1]

Temujin's people emerged from forests lying along the northern edges of Mongolia. They had been hunter-gatherers, surviving on the animals they could kill and the plants they could collect. It was a very uncertain way of life. If the hunter-gatherers' food disappeared, they would die.

Hunter-gatherers often became farmers after settling by rivers and lakes. Growing crops was easier when the land was near a good source of water.

The Mongolian people settled between the Onon and Kherlen Rivers. Unfortunately, the rivers are frozen half of the year. When it is not freezing cold, it is incredibly hot. Summer days are often over 100 degrees Fahrenheit. The area is also landlocked; the closest ocean is hundreds of miles away.

Instead of planting crops, the Mongols raised cattle and sheep. They were nomads—traveling from place to place with no permanent home. They lived in tents called yurts. Their herds ate a lot of grass. The Mongols did not grow food for their animals, so when their animals had eaten all the grass, they moved on.

They did not own the land. They used what they needed.

In the forest, people were able to survive on their own. But along the Steppes, the Mongols relied on each other for protection. Groups formed to defend their animals and the land they needed from outsiders. These small groups of people were called clans.

These nomadic herdsmen relied on one animal more than any other—the horse. On horseback, the Mongols could travel great distances quickly. They became fearsome fighters, experts with bows and arrows. They could fire accurately from atop their horses. They were deadly with other weapons like the sword and the spear. But as Temujin was growing up, the Mongolian clans mainly fought each other.

**Yesugei**

Temujin's father, Yesugei, was not a khan. A khan was a king of an entire nation, but Yesugei was just the leader of the **Borjigins**, a clan that was considered royalty. Yesugei was very powerful. He often took whatever he wanted, including another man's wife.

While traveling, he noticed a man riding on horseback, followed by a woman in a cart. Yesugei crept closer for a better look. And in that moment, he fell in love. Turning his horse, he raced home and got his two brothers.

Yesugei and his brothers then rode quickly back to the traveling pair.

The woman Yesugei and his brothers took was named Hoelun. The man riding in front of her, **Chiledu**, was her husband and also the brother of the **Merkit** chief. She told Chiledu that he should give her to Yesugei. If he didn't, Yesugei and his brothers would kill him. Besides, she explained, there would be other women. She wasn't worth dying for.

Chiledu fled, but Yesugei had made a powerful enemy—not just for himself, but for his family. The Merkit never forgot.

**Hoelun**

When the boy who became Genghis Khan was born sometime around 1165, his tiny hand clutched a clot of blood. Yesugei believed it was a sign that his son would be a great warrior.

His parents named him Temujin. He was named after a man his father had captured—Temujin-uge, the chief of the Tartars.

Like many Mongolian boys, Temujin learned to ride a horse while he was still learning how to walk. Mongolian children were comfortable with horses even before they could hold on to a bridle.

By the age of five, Temujin was learning how to use a bow and arrow for hunting and fighting. It was an important skill. Mongolia was a dangerous place. Clan fought clan; family fought family. When the groups were not killing each other, they were stealing from each other. Yesugei's conflict with the Tartars may have killed him. Before he was ten years old, Temujin lost his dad, and Hoelun had seven children to raise alone. Temujin wanted to be a leader like his father, but instead, he was starving.

No one helped. Not his father's family nor his mother's. **Kiriltuk**, a member of the **Taychiut** family, saw the chance to take over as leader and he didn't hesitate. Rallying the other clan members, he rode off, expecting Temujin and his family to starve to death.

Instead, Temujin learned to make his own hooks to catch fish. His mother foraged for nuts and berries in the woods. The family survived harsh winters and brutal summers. And he turned a friend into a brother.

At nine, Temujin had met the girl he would marry. At ten, Temujin became *anda*—blood brothers—with the boy who would help save her life. **Jamukha** was about the same age as Temujin, and they had grown up together. They hunted and fished together. They traded arrows. Then they agreed to become blood brothers. To make the brotherhood official, they gave each other the knucklebones of sheep. The bones were used as dice in a traditional Mongolian game called knucklebones (or ***shagai***).

Unfortunately, Temujin was having problems with his real blood relations. Like many blended families where the brothers and sisters have different parents, there were conflicts between Yesugei's children. Instead of yelling or complaining, Temujin got even.

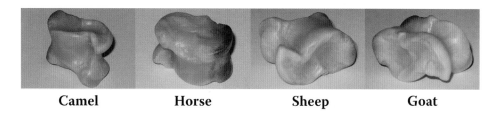

| Camel | Horse | Sheep | Goat |

**Children and families play games with sheep ankle bones called *shagai*. The bones can land on one of four sides: horse (mor), camel (temee), goat (yamaa), or sheep (khon). There are several versions of this game. In one version, players flick the shagai into one another, trying to hit two bones of the same type together. Players get to keep matching bones, or lose a turn if they hit a bone that doesn't match. The object is to collect as many bones as possible.**

# The Yurt

The Mongols lived in a type of tent called a yurt. After turning sheep's wool into felt, the felt was stretched over a circular wooden frame. The Mongols had plenty of sheep, but they had to trade with outsiders for wood.

The yurt was kept warm by an open fire in the center. A hole in the center of the yurt's ceiling provided an escape for the smoke. The door was typically a flap cut from the felt. A floor was sometimes constructed from wooden planks.

The yurt was the perfect home for a nomad. It could be taken down or put back up in about two hours. It was carried on the backs of camels or horses—usually two or three animals were required to move the parts of the yurt.

The yurt was decorated on the inside with clan symbols. Today, campers can stay in yurts in state parks across the United States.

Perhaps the best horsemen that ever lived, the Mongols could ride sideways or backward and accurately fire an arrow. This portrait of Genghis Khan at the Brooklyn Museum shows the leader astride a horse—he probably learned to ride not long after he learned to walk.

# CHAPTER 3
## Captive!

Temujin grew up learning how to be a Mongolian. In addition to riding a horse and using a bow and arrow, he learned to share.

In the bleak land where Mongolians lived, members of a clan usually helped each other out. When one member caught a fish or killed an animal, they shared it with the clan. Sharing his treasure with other men would be part of the reason that one day Temujin would lead thousands.

But instead of sharing, Temujin's brothers Bekter and Belgutei took. When Temujin and his brother Kasar caught fish or killed birds, Bekter and Belgutei stole them.

Although Yesugei was the father of all four boys, **Bekter** and **Belgutei** had a different mother. After his death, the children did not have enough to eat. Temujin was around fourteen years old, and Bekter was probably a little older when Temujin and **Kasar** complained to their mother. Hoelun didn't do anything.

*The Secret History of the Mongols* reports that Temujin asked, "How can we live together?" He went outside with his eleven-year-old brother Kasar. They both crept to where Bekter was guarding the family's horses. "Temujin [crept] up from behind while Kasar [crept] up from in front." They raised their bows and arrows. "Temujin and Kasar shot at him from in front and from behind. . . ."[1]

Bekter died instantly.

Hoelun was angry. But it was not his mother that Temujin had to worry about. Kiriltuk, the Taychiut leader, soon came looking for Temujin.

At that time in Mongolia, many people got away with murder. Still, some stories say that the killing is the reason that the Taychiut attacked the family's camp. Others suspect that Kiriltuk noticed Temujin growing tall and strong. Anyone who would kill his half-brother for stealing fish was someone to be feared.

Kiriltuk and his Taychiut clan surrounded Hoelun's tents. They only wanted Temujin. They promised her the family would be unharmed.

Hearing Temujin's name, his family helped him escape into the woods. He hid there for over a week, cold and hungry. He almost starved to death before he finally surrendered.

Kiriltuk imprisoned Temujin. He was held in a wooden collar attached to his neck and wrists. This painful device was called a cangue. He wore it night and day. It made it difficult to sleep or to eat. A guard kept him from escaping by holding a rope which was strung around his neck. Temujin was transferred from one home to another as the Taychiut families took turns watching over the prisoner. When Temujin stayed with a man named **Sorkan**, the family loosened the cangue at night so Temujin could sleep more comfortably.

Each summer, Mongolians held a festival called "Red Circle Day." During the festival, almost everyone in the Taychiut camp was celebrating, leaving only a puny teenager to watch over Temujin. He had one chance and he took it.

Temujin hit the guard in the head with his cangue. Then he ran.

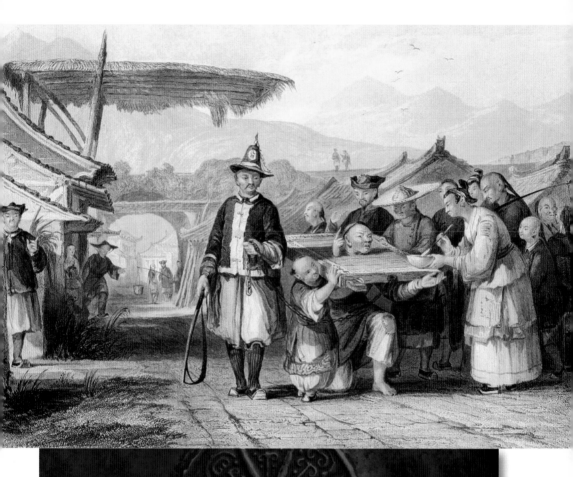

Cumbersome and uncomfortable, the cangue made it difficult to sleep or eat, let alone escape. Temujin figured out a way to use it as a weapon.

Temujin leaped into the chilly Onon River. He floated beneath the river with only his head above the water. Soon the Taychiuts began searching for him. Sorkan was walking home along the river and saw Temujin. He told Temujin to stay hidden while the Taychiuts searched. Later, he hid him in his home and gave him warm clothes and a horse.

Temujin rode as fast as he could toward his mother's tent.

Nothing a Mongolian owned was as important as their horse. A year after Temujin's escape from the Taychiut clan, thieves took eight of his family's nine horses. When his brother returned from hunting with the ninth one, Temujin climbed on and sped after them.

He rode for three days. He was almost as exhausted as his horse when he saw a tent. Temujin stopped. He was greeted by **Boorchu**, a thirteen-year-old boy who had seen the thieves. Noticing how tired Temujin's horse was, Boorchu insisted that he take one of his family's horses. He also wanted to help. "All men's sufferings are common," he said. "I will come with you."[2]

For three more days, they trailed the thieves, following the horses' tracks. Finally the pair reached them. When the thieves saw Temujin and Boorchu escaping with the horses, they chased them. One of the thieves came close and Temujin fired an arrow. Finally, the two managed to lose the thieves.

Looking at the horses, Temujin offered several to Boorchu, but the boy refused.

Back at home, Boorchu's father was very angry. His son had never told him he was leaving. He was afraid his son had been kidnapped.

Boorchu told his father that he'd been with Temujin and explained what had happened. Although Boorchu's father was still upset, he liked Temujin. He told his son to stay with Temujin and to return to Temujin's family. Boorchu became one of Temujin's best generals.

Not long afterward, Temujin left his home again. He planned to marry the girl he'd met when he was nine. But would her parents honor their promise? Would Börte even remember him?

Temujin's worries were pointless. Her parents were still happy to have Temujin as a son-in-law. As for Börte, she was seventeen years old. Most girls her age had been married for years, but she had waited.

Temujin was the only boy she'd ever loved. The family gave Temujin a very expensive sable coat as a present for his mother. Instead, the coat would save Temujin's young bride.

# Religion

Shamanism is a religion that many Mongols practiced in Genghis Khan's time. People who follow shamanism believe that the world is inhabited by spirits. Some are gods, with the power to help or harm. But everything has a spirit—even a rock, a river, or an arrow.

Mongols like Genghis Khan believed in the highest god called Eternal Blue Heaven, the creator of the world. Mongols also believed in other gods like **Qurmusata**, the creator of fire. Since fire was sacred to the Mongols, they would not stamp it out or put water on it.

A **shaman** was similar to a priest, and could communicate with the spirit world, or read signs in things like animal bones. Their prayers could make it rain or thunder.

Although Genghis Khan practiced shamanism, he was tolerant of other beliefs. After invading a country, he allowed the people to practice their own religions. He even studied their religions, hoping to learn whatever new ideas he could. Genghis grew his empire in part because he welcomed those people whose leaders had banished them because of their religion.

The life and military victories of Genghis Khan are studied across the world, but in Mongolia, he is held in especially high regard. This memorial is located near the capital, Ulaanbaatar.

# CHAPTER 4
# The Battle Begins

Temujin was finally married to the girl he'd met when he was nine years old. He'd made new friends and escaped old enemies. Now he wanted to do what his father couldn't. He wanted to unite the warring Mongolian clans.

Because he couldn't do it alone, Temujin went to **Toghrul**. The leader of the powerful **Kereit** clan had been Yesugei's blood brother. Temujin considered Toghrul to be like a second father. When he arrived, he offered Toghrul the fur coat. "In return for the black sable jacket," Toghrul said, "I will bring together the people who abandoned you."[1]

Happy with this promise, Temujin returned home. It was a good thing he'd made a new ally. He would soon need one.

Although both Chiledu and Yesugei were now dead, the Merkit had never forgotten how Hoelun had been stolen. When they heard about Temujin's new wife, they prepared to take revenge. Three hundred of them attacked Temujin's camp.

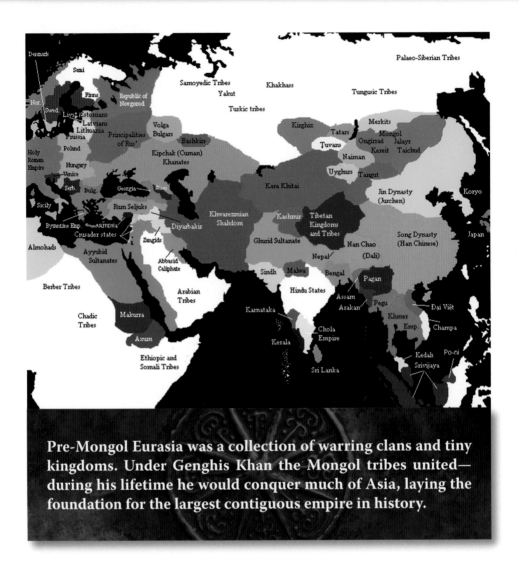

Pre-Mongol Eurasia was a collection of warring clans and tiny kingdoms. Under Genghis Khan the Mongol tribes united—during his lifetime he would conquer much of Asia, laying the foundation for the largest contiguous empire in history.

Temujin's mother and his siblings escaped. Börte was kidnapped. She was made the wife of Chiledu's younger brother.

Temujin hid out on Burkhan Khaldun Mountain until the Merkit left. He said, "I escaped, sparing mine only life with an only horse." Because he believed the mountain saved his life, he promised to pray to it every day and teach his children to do the same.[2]

Temujin went back to see Toghrul. He promised to "crush the Merkits and rescue Lady Börte for you."[3]

Temujin's blood brother Jamukha also helped. Both Toghrul and Jamukha commanded thousands of men.

The battle got off to a bad start. Jamukha waited three days for Temujin and Toghrul. He'd brought about twenty thousand soldiers and twice as many horses. They were running out of food.

When Toghrul and Temujin arrived, Jamukha was furious. Temujin listened as his blood brother yelled. "Even if a snowstorm stands in the way of the appointment, even if rain hinders the meeting, we [should] not be late. Did we not so agree?"[4]

Toghrul and Temujin both knew he was right and apologized. Then they made a battle plan.

A week later, the army reached the Merkit camp alongside the **Khilok** River. At nightfall, they attacked. The Merkits were not ready. Most of them ran. Those who stayed and fought, died.

Temujin drove his horse through the fighting Mongols. As he did, he screamed for Börte. She was in a cart, racing away with the fleeing Merkits. When she heard her husband's voice, she jumped from the moving cart and ran. When Temujin's horse reached her, she grabbed its reins.

Moments later, husband and wife were in each other's arms. Temujin told everyone not to chase the Merkits—he didn't need to go after them. He had gotten what he'd come for.

The Merkits left their riches at the camp. Temujin offered most of his share to the men in their army.

Toghrul returned to his camp, but Temujin stayed with Jamukha. They fought together, winning small battles with rival tribes. Jamukha's soldiers quickly realized that Temujin's men got to keep more of the treasure than they did. Temujin did not care about a soldier's clan. He gave everyone the chance to be a leader.

After a year and a half of traveling together, Jamukha told Temujin they needed to separate. Temujin was crushed, but Börte understood. "Jamukha is said to [become easily bored]," she told her husband. "The time has come for him to [become bored] of us. . . . Rather than pitch camp, we should continue on our journey." They kept going through the night, leaving Jamukha and his army behind.[5]

As Temujin put miles between himself and his blood brother, he noticed something. Many of Jamukha's soldiers had followed. They came from lesser clans like the **Tarkut**, **Mangut**, and Suldu. They wanted him to be their leader—their khan.

During a ceremony in 1186, he was elected khan of the Borjigin clan.

While Temujin was still in his twenties, he became a powerful khan. Still, there were other powerful khans in Mongolia. Jamukha was one of them. Not long after they separated, Temujin's blood brother was ready to kill him.

Around 1187, a man stole an entire herd of horses belonging to one of Temujin's men. The soldier chased the thief and killed him, recovering his horses. Unfortunately, the horse thief was Jamukha's brother. It did not matter that there was a good reason for his death. Jamukha declared war.

Temujin lost the Battle of Dalan Balzhut against Jamukha. He retreated, hiding out in a valley. Jamukha ordered that Temujin's captured soldiers be boiled alive.

No one knows for sure what happened next. Some people suggest that Temujin spent the following years south of Mongolia in China. What is known is that by 1196, Temujin had joined forces with the Chinese to battle a common enemy.

The Tartars didn't get along very well with their neighbors, in part because they stole from them on a regular basis. Temujin and Toghrul came together. While the Chinese attacked the Tartars from the front, Temujin and Toghrul attacked from the rear. By the time the two armies met, the Tartars had been slaughtered.

Afterward, Toghrul was named "Wang Khan" (King) by the Chinese leader, General Wanyan Xiang. Temujin was named a military commander.

Genghis Khan met both his wife and one his greatest enemies while he was still a child. Temujin and Jamukha became blood brothers as children, but as adults they were dangerous rivals.

The conflict had other rewards. The Tartar property helped make Temujin rich. He also adopted a small Tartar boy, who would be raised by Hoelun. In future battles, Temujin would often adopt the children of the men he'd killed in battle. After battles, he did not execute enemy soldiers but instead offered them a chance to fight with him. His army grew very quickly this way.

In the battle against the Tartars, Temujin learned how the Chinese fought. There were only two million people in Mongolia. China had over one hundred million. Yet Temujin soon dreamed of defeating them.

Here Wang Khan is shown dressed as a Cardinal with his attendants to the right holding crosses. Some people in the West believed that Wang Khan was Prester John, a Christian king in the East who may have been nothing more than a legend.

# Military Training Under Genghis Khan

Although often outnumbered, Genghis Khan's army still won most of the battles it fought. One reason was that he organized his army better than his enemies did.

He began by assembling the best fighters. Those became his bodyguards or **keshig**. Eventually he had ten thousand of them. Many were the sons or brothers of his military leaders. This reduced the risk of desertion—soldiers leaving his army. A father would not want to leave his son behind.

Genghis also organized ten-man squads (*Aravs*) with a leader. Ten of these squads formed a hundred-man company (a *Zuut*). The company also had a leader as did the battalion force (a *Minghan*) of ten companies or one thousand men. Ten thousand men, or ten battalions, was a *Tumen*.

The soldiers all came from different clans, but fought side-by-side. They took orders from leaders who came from different clans—even clans they had once fought against. At the height of his power, Genghis Khan required every able-bodied adult male Mongol to join his army. It would number over one hundred thousand soldiers.

**Mongol warriors**

Far older than Genghis Khan, the Great Wall of China took hundreds of years to complete. Designed to keep out "barbarians," today it is visible from space.

# CHAPTER 5
## Over the Wall

The Great Wall of China can be seen from space. Constructed over hundreds of years, much of it was already built centuries before Temujin's birth. Running thousands of miles along the Chinese-Mongolian border, the wall was supposed to keep out nomads like the Mongols. The Chinese called them barbarians.

Temujin wanted to lead his people against the rich country to the south. But first, he would have to unite the Mongols—which meant defeating the other khans.

In 1201, Jamukha became the leader of many clans—including Tartar and Merkit warriors who hated Temujin and Wang Khan. After they elected Jamukha "**Gur** Khan," he was ready to eliminate his rivals.

The next year, Gur Khan's forces attacked Temujin's army. Temujin fought back and sent messengers to Wang Khan to tell him about the attack. Wang Khan brought his men to help.

During the Battle of Koyitan, one of Gur Khan's priests prayed for a storm to rain over Temujin's men. A thunderstorm did begin soon after. It turned the ground to mud. Instead of stopping the enemy, the storm followed Gur Khan's men until they could barely move. Temujin's army was higher up. It was easy to hit the slow-moving soldiers with arrows.

After Temujin won the battle, his blood brother fled.

The victory was brief. Fighting against the Taychiut, Temujin was shot in the neck with a poison arrow. He almost died. His blood began to clot and one of his men had to suck the blood out of his neck to save his life.

The next year, Temujin tried to strengthen the relationship between his people and the Wang Khan's people. He had a suggestion for the Wang Khan's son, **Senggum**. Temujin wanted his son to marry Senggum's sister; in exchange, Temujin's daughter would marry Senggum's son. But Senggum had other ideas. He thought that his people were better than Temujin's people, and was insulted by the offer.

Then, Senggum set a trap. He lied to Temujin, sending word that he had changed his mind, and his sister would marry Temujin's son. He asked Temujin to come to a celebration. Senggum planned to capture the Mongol leader.

Temujin was excited and headed out to join the celebration. But before he arrived, one of his men became suspicious of the sudden change, and told Temujin to send spies ahead. When the spies warned him about the plot, Temujin fled.

In 1203, he organized his army and prepared for war. Wang Khan refused Temujin's peace offer.

The battle was brutal, but in the end Temujin won and his former friend Wang Khan was killed. With this victory, Temujin was now the ruler of Wang Khan's Kereit clan.

In 1206, Temujin finally defeated Gur Khan and his army. The leader was captured by his own men and brought before Temujin. The men who captured Gur Khan were executed—Temujin believed

The news of Wang Khan's death spread quickly to other clans. Here, his head is brought to Tayang Khan of the Naimans as proof of his death.

he couldn't trust any man who would betray his own leader. As for Gur Khan, he was offered the chance to join Temujin again as his blood brother. But Gur Khan refused. He admitted that he had left Temujin years ago because he was jealous. It was too late now to fix what he had done. He asked only that he be killed honorably, without his blood being spilled. Temujin agreed.

Following these victories, Temujin was elected "Genghis Khan." The leader was illiterate—he could not read or write. He knew that with a large army he would have to write down orders. He also needed to write down rules.

Genghis Khan had a writing system developed for the Mongol language. This system used the **Uighur** alphabet, which was adopted from the Uighur people he had conquered. He also created a set of

Temujin is named "Genghis Khan," as his sons Jochi and Ögodei (right) look on.

laws called yasa. Stealing, killing, and a number of other crimes were punished by death. The harsh laws created an obedient society as the once-warring Mongol clans began to work together.

His men needed to be well organized. They planned to invade areas they had never fought in before.

For five years, Genghis Khan and his well-trained soldiers attacked the Tanguts. Their kingdom lay beside the Yellow River in a part of China where the Inner Mongolia Region is today. The Mongols needed more animals and the Tanguts seemed like the perfect people to steal them from. But like the Chinese, the Tanguts protected their land with walls. These battles marked the first time that the Mongols had fought against a walled city.

On the other side of Tangut land lay China. Many of Genghis's men followed him because of the treasure they received when they fought. If Genghis didn't keep invading foreign lands, his men might leave. China's riches were legendary, and Genghis soon realized that defeating the Tanguts once and for all would give them a clear path to enter China.

So the Mongols tried different ideas to get past the Tanguts' walls. In one battle, they pretended to flee, causing the Tanguts to come out from their city. Once the Tanguts were outside of the protection of their walls, the Mongols turned and attacked. In the final battle, Genghis built a dam which would flood the Tangut city. Just as it looked like the Tanguts could not possibly win, the dam broke, flooding the Mongols instead. Genghis had to settle for a peace agreement.

Nonetheless, Genghis had secured the Tangut land and was ready to take on the Jin rulers in China. In 1211, his forces crossed the outer walls which protected the famous Great Wall of China. Within two years, Genghis Khan and his army had reached the capital of **Zhongdu** (Beijing).

In most battles, Genghis Khan allowed survivors to join his army. In his wars against the Jin, there were not any survivors. The Mongols

Pavel Ryzhenko's painting, *The Battle of Kalka*, illustrates Genghis Khan and his army invading Russia.

Genghis Khan and his army fought the Khwarezmid Empire at the Indus River in 1221. With their victory there, the Mongols added the Khwarezmid land to their empire.

killed everyone they found. The Jin imperial palace burned for days. Although his men destroyed the cities, he did not kill as many in northern China. Instead, he collected taxes from the people.

For another fourteen years, Genghis Khan and his Mongols invaded some of the richest and most powerful kingdoms on earth. They defeated Persia, where Iran and Afghanistan are today. They defeated the Russians who fought them in Ukraine. His army grew as the gold, silver, and other riches they took became legendary.

In 1226, Genghis Khan was injured while he was out hunting on horseback. According to some sources, he never recovered from his

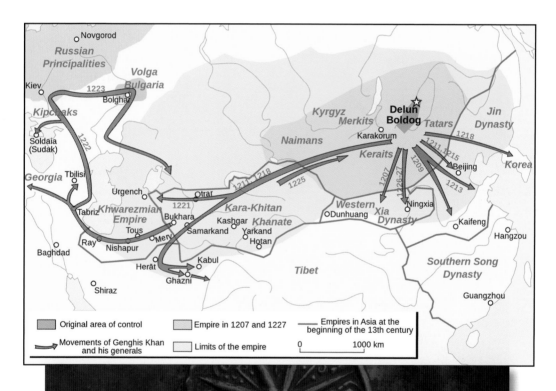

**Genghis Khan and his heirs oversaw a growing kingdom, one that was rich and powerful. Much of Asia was under Mongol control by the time of Genghis's death in 1227.**

injuries. Others say he became ill. But the sources do agree that he died in August of 1227.

He had united the Mongols, providing them with an empire and a set of laws. The kingdoms of other famous rulers like Napoleon and Alexander the Great fell apart after they died. The empire Genghis Khan created endured. Before he died, he chose his son **Ögodei** as the new khan. He asked his other sons to support Ögodei instead of dividing and fighting. The empire could only survive if they were united. His sons and grandsons expanded their rule across Asia, Europe, and the Middle East. At its peak, the Mongol Empire was the largest in the world. It was an empire that left a legacy that would live on in stories and history books for hundreds of years after Genghis Khan's death.

**After the death of Genghis Khan, his son Ögodei became khan.**

# Polo

Today many people see polo as a game for the rich. It is a game played on horseback. One team tries to score by hitting a ball through the other team's goal using 4½ foot mallets.

The game was played by the Mongols when Genghis Khan was their leader. It is easy to see why. The Mongol army relied on its cavalry—soldiers mounted on horseback. Polo was a good way to train them. If they could get around an opponent in a game of polo, they could do the same thing on a battlefield.

Polo began in Asia. No one is certain when it was invented. Some believe it was first played in Persia over 2,500 years ago. Written records show that the game was being played throughout Asia 2,000 years ago.

**This mid-sixteenth-century painting illustrates the game of polo.**

**CE**

**ca. 1165**  Born in Mongolia, the boy who became Genghis Khan was named Temujin.

**1174**  Temujin meets Börte. His father is killed soon after.

**1179**  After Temujin's half-brother, Bekter, steals his food, Temujin and his brother Kasar shoot him with arrows. The Taychiuts raid Temujin's camp and take him prisoner.

**1182**  Temujin marries Börte.

**1183**  The Merkit tribe steals Börte; Temujin teams up with Toghrul and Jamukha to take her back.

**1186**  Temujin is elected Borjigin Khan.

**1187**  Loses the Battle of Dalan Balzhut to Jamukha.

**1196**  Together with Toghrul and the Chinese, Temujin defeats the Tartars. Toghrul is named Wang Khan.

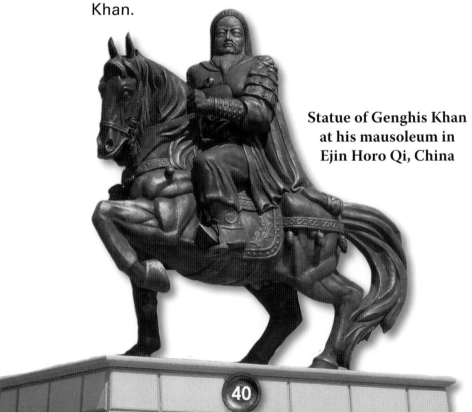

**Statue of Genghis Khan at his mausoleum in Ejin Horo Qi, China**

| 1201 | Jamukha is named "Gur Khan." |
|---|---|
| 1202 | Temujin and Toghrul defeat Jamukha in the Battle of Koyitan. Temujin destroys the Tartar villages, killing the men while enslaving the women and children. |
| 1203 | Temujin battles Toghrul; Temujin takes over the Kereit throne after Toghrul is killed. |
| 1206 | Completes his conquest of Mongolia and is proclaimed emperor of all Mongols—the Genghis Khan. |
| 1213 | Conquers the Jin Empire in Northern China and occupies its capital, Zhongdu (Beijing). |
| 1220 | The Mongols conquer Persia. |
| 1223 | Defeats Russians in present-day Ukraine. |
| 1227 | Genghis Khan dies of an injury or illness. |

Ghengis Khan Mausoleum near Ordos in Inner Mongolia

**CE**

**613**     Muhammad begins teaching Islam in the Middle East.

**795**     Vikings attack the island monastery of Iona, Scotland.

**954**     The last Viking king in England, Eric Bloodaxe, is killed. The Vikings are driven from York.

**1040**     After defeating Duncan I of Scotland, Macbeth becomes king.

**1044**     The *Wujing Zongyao* is written in China, detailing instructions for making gunpowder and flamethrowers.

**ca. 1096**     The University of Oxford is founded.

**1115**     The Jin Dynasty is founded in northern China.

**1170**     Thomas Becket, the Archbishop of Canterbury, is killed by King Henry II's soldiers.

**1215**     The Magna Carta is signed at Runnymede, the first document limiting royal power in England.

**1241**     Mongols invade Eastern Europe, attacking the lands where Poland, Hungary, and Croatia are today.

**1258**     Mongols invade and destroy Baghdad.

**1260**     Ariq Böke (Genghis's grandson) challenges his brother Kublai Khan for control of the Mongol Empire.

**1275–1292** Marco Polo serves at the court of Kublai Khan.

**1368** The Ming Dynasty overthrows the Mongols in China.

Genghis (Chinggis) Kahn (d. 1227)
Jochi (d. 1227)
Ogodei (r. 1229–41)
Chaghadai (d. 1242)
Tolui (d. 1233)
Guyug (r. 1246–48)
Batu (d. 1255)
Berke
Mongke (r. 1251–59)
Khublai (r. 1260–94)
Hulegu (d. 1265)
Arigh Boke

**THE MONGOL KHANS DYNASTY**

Genghis Khan's family tree. The row just above Genghis shows his four sons. The others are his grandsons. The letter "d" indicates the person's date of death, while "r" indicates the years that person ruled.

## Chapter 1

1. Francis Woodman Cleaves, translator, *The Secret History of the Mongols* (Cambridge, MA: Harvard-Yenching Institute by Harvard University Press, 1982), pp. 15, 17.
2. Ibid.
3. John Man, *Genghis Khan: Life, Death, and Resurrection* (New York: Thomas Dunne Books/St. Martin's Press, 2004), p. 36.

## Chapter 2

1. John Man, *Genghis Khan: Life, Death, and Resurrection* (New York: Thomas Dunne Books/St. Martin's Press, 2004), p. 38.

## Chapter 3

1. Francis Woodman Cleaves, translator, *The Secret History of the Mongols* (Cambridge, MA: Harvard-Yenching Institute by Harvard University Press, 1982), pp. 22–23.
2. John Man, *Genghis Khan: Life, Death, and Resurrection* (New York: Thomas Dunne Books/St. Martin's Press, 2004), p. 80.

## Chapter 4

1. Urgunge Onon, translator, *The Secret History of the Mongols* (New York: RoutledgeCurzon, 2001), p. 80.
2. Francis Woodman Cleaves, translator, *The Secret History of the Mongols* (Cambridge, MA: Harvard-Yenching Institute by Harvard University Press, 1982), pp. 36–37.
3. Urgunge Onon, translator, *The Secret History of the Mongols* (New York: RoutledgeCurzon, 2001), p. 86.
4. Ibid., p. 91.
5. Ibid., p. 99.

## Books
Burgan, Michael. *Empire of the Mongols*. New York: Chelsea House, 2009.

Kent, Zachary. *Genghis Khan: Invincible Ruler of the Mongol Empire*. Berkeley Heights, NJ: Enslow Publishers, 2008.

Nardo, Don. *Life During the Great Civilizations: The Mongol Empire*. Farmington Hills, MI: Blackbirch Press, 2005.

Rice, Earle, Jr. *Empire in the East: The Story of Genghis Khan*. Greensboro, NC: Morgan Reynolds, 2005.

## On the Internet
Biography.com: "Genghis Khan"
http://www.biography.com/people/genghis-khan-9308634

Kidipede: "Mongol Empire"
http://www.historyforkids.org/learn/centralasia/history/mongols.htm

KidsPast.com: "Genghis Khan"
http://www.kidspast.com/world-history/0236-genghis-khan.php

## Works Consulted

Bodrov, Sergei. *Mongol*. DVD. New Line Home Entertainment, 2007.

Cleaves, Francis Woodman, translator. *The Secret History of the Mongols.* Cambridge, MA: Harvard-Yenching Institute by Harvard University Press, 1982.

Hartog, Leo de. *Genghis Khan, Conqueror of the World*. New York: St. Martin's Press, 1989.

Komaroff, Linda, and Stefano Carboni. *The Legacy of Genghis Khan: Courtly Art and Culture in Western Asia, 1256–1353*. New York: Metropolitan Museum of Art, 2002.

Man, John. *Genghis Khan: Life, Death, and Resurrection*. New York: Thomas Dunne Books/St. Martin's Press, 2004.

Mongoluls.net: "A History of Religion in Mongolia."
http://mongoluls.net/mongolian-religion/monrelihis.shtml

Onon, Urgunge, translator. *The Secret History of the Mongols*. New York: RoutledgeCurzon, 2001.

Ratchnevsky, Paul. *Genghis Khan: His Life and Legacy*. Oxford, UK: Blackwell, 1991.

Stewart, Stanley. *In the Empire of Genghis Khan*. Guilford, CT: Lyons Press, 2002.

# PHONETIC PRONUNCIATIONS

Bekter (BEG-ter)

Belgutei (BELL-geh-tay)

Boorchu (BOH-ohr-choo)

Borjigin (BOR-zhig-ihn)

Börte (BOR-tuh)

Burkhan Khaldun (BAHR-khen KHAHL-doon)

Chiledu (CHIH-leh-doo)

Genghis (JENG-gis)

Gur (GOOR)

Hoelun (HO-eh-loon)

Indus (IN-duhs) Jamukha (JAH-moo-kuh)

Jochi (JAH-chee)

Kalka (KAL-kuh)

Kasar (KAH-sahr)

Kazakhstan (kah-zahk-STAHN)

Kereit (KAIR-ayt)

keshig (KEH-shihg)

Khan (KAHN)

Kherlen (KAIR-uh-lan)

Khilok (khi-LOHK)

Khwarezmid (KWAHR-ehz-mihd)

Kiriltuk (KEER-eel-tugkh)

Mangut (MAHN-ghoodt)

Merkit (MEHR-keedt)

Mongol (MONG-guhl)

Naiman (NAI-mahn)

Ögodei (AHG-uh-day)

Qurmusata (KHOOR-moo-sah-tah)

Senggum (SEHN-goohm)

shagai (SHAH-guy)

shaman (SHAH-muhn)

Shigi (SHEE-gee)

Sorkan (SHOR-gahn)

Tarkut (TAHR-koot)

Taychiut (TIE-chee-oodt)

Temujin (tehm-OO-jin)

Toghrul (TOHG-rihl)

Uighur (WEE-goor)

Ulaanbaatar (OO-lahn-BAH-tah)

Yesugei (yih-SOO-gay)

Zhongdu (ZHONG-doo)

**PHOTO CREDITS:** Cover, pp. 1, 4, 6, 8, 10, 11, 12, 13, 14, 17, 19, 20, 22, 25, 26, 27, 31, 34–35, 36, 37, 38, 39, 41, 43; pp. 28, 47—Photos.com; p. 32—DeAgostini/Getty Images. Every effort has been made to locate all copyright holders of materials used in this book. Any errors or omissions will be corrected in future editions of the book.

**ally** (AL-ahy)—A person or country that works together with another person or country.

**anda**—A blood brother in Mongol culture.

**barbarian** (bahr-BAIR-ee-uhn)—An uncivilized person.

**cangue** (KANG)—A wooden collar used to hold prisoners.

**cavalry** (KAV-uhl-ree)—The section of an army made up of soldiers fighting on horseback.

**execution** (ek-si-KYOO-shuhn)—The killing of a criminal as punishment for their crimes.

**illiterate** (ih-LIT-er-it)—Not able to read or write.

**khan** (KAHN)—The king or highest leader of Mongol tribes.

**siege** (SEEJ)—The surrounding of an area in order to force the people to surrender.

**yurt** (YOORT)—A circular tent that was used as a home for Mongols.

Statue of Genghis Khan in front of the Mongolian government building in Sükhbaatar Square, Ulaanbaatar

47